ARTIFICERS & ALCHEMY

DUNGEONS & DRAGONS

ARTIFICERS & ALCHEMY

A Young Adventurer's Guide

WRITTEN BY JIM ZUB AND STACY KING

WITH ANDREW WHEELER

TEN SPEED PRESS
California | New York

CONTENTS

CURIOUS CONSTRUCTS 49

ARTIFICERS 69

DESIGNING YOUR OWN MAGIC ITEMS 85

INTRODUCTION

Magic is an important part of any fantasy story. It creates colorful and exciting moments that can inspire us. Spells are a fantastic part of every caster's toolkit, but unusual items or places imbued with magical power can be even more impressive. How are those enchanted objects created? What rare magic items, constructs, or other phenomena can be found in the worlds of DUNGEONS & DRAGONS?

This book will answer those questions and unlock a multitude of arcane secrets for you to explore. It's a guide to the weird and wondrous ways that magic is used to transform the everyday into the extraordinary—wild weapons, exceptional equipment, and potent prosthetics as well as tremendous tomes, lavish locales, and curious constructs.

You can read this guide from beginning to end in one sitting, or open it up at any spot, be drawn in by the exciting illustrations, and let inspiration take you somewhere special. The more you read, the more ideas for mythic gear, infused instruments, and peculiar phenomena you'll discover!

Will your adventurers be empowered by the strange sorcery they encounter, or will those powers be too much for them to handle? That's up to you. The magic of DUNGEONS & DRAGONS begins here on the page, but where the fantastical story goes is only limited by your imagination.

Let's make some magic!

ENCHANTED ITEMS

When Hilne and Flix had taken the job of "liberating" a certain spellbook from Mossclover Castle, their wizard client had promised that the guards were pushovers. The glowing red eyes and shadowed face of the library sentinel said otherwise. Flix wanted to quit on the spot, but a quick inventory review produced a better plan. Hilne would use her magic reveler's concertina to enchant the guard, while Flix snuck past him unseen using his dust of disappearance. They just hoped that the guard's dancing wouldn't be so funny that Flix gave himself away with an ill-timed giggle!

The variety of magic items available in your adventure is as vast as your imagination. Some items unleash supernatural effects so grand they can't be overlooked, while other objects deliver their magic in subtle yet powerful ways. Throughout this book you'll discover enchanted creations from across the worlds of D&D, including legendary weapons, guardian gear, and curative contraptions powerful enough to have minds of their own.

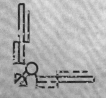
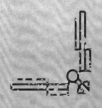

LEGENDARY WEAPONS

L egendary weapons exceed the usual benefits of magical weapons, delivering extraordinary powers worthy of the most illustrious adventurers. These armaments must be attuned to their user, forming a mystical bond, which means that only one adventurer can access the weapon's magic. In some cases this bond can flow both ways, causing the user to take on traits associated with the item's magic.

LUCK BLADE Every *luck blade* is infused with good fortune. Once per day, you can use the blade's luck to instantly retry a failed attempt to use the sword, giving you a second chance at success. Every *luck blade* contains up to three uses of a *wish* spell, the most powerful magic any mortal can wield. The *luck blade* retains the rest of its magic once its *wish* spells are used up. *Luck blades* can be greatswords, longswords, rapiers, scimitars, or shortswords.

NINE LIVES STEALER These blades are both cherished and feared by adventurers who seek to battle the most mighty of monsters, for legends are told of their ability to slay formidable beasts with a single blow. A *nine lives stealer* will, in the right circumstances, attempt to draw out the life force of its target. Should the blade succeed, the creature is instantly slain. This ability can only be used nine times for each sword. Characters who value goodness and morality may feel uncomfortable using the soul-shattering magic of a *nine lives stealer*.

TINDERSTRIKE This uncommonly sharp dagger contains a shard of Imix, the Prince of Evil Fire. The handle is always warm, and the blade smolders like hot coals for several minutes after each use. *Tinderstrike* grants fire mastery, allowing its holder to speak the language of fire elementals, command them, and resist fire damage. Within magical locations called *fire nodes*, the dagger can be used to create an elemental explosive device known as a devastation orb. Attunement to *Tinderstrike* makes its wielder impatient and rash, causing them to act without thinking and take needless risks until the magical bond is broken.

QUIVER OF EHLONNA Named for the goddess of woodlands in the realm of Greyhawk, this magic archer's case is especially prized by druids, although any adventurer may be attuned to it. The *quiver of Ehlonna's* three compartments connect to an extradimensional space, allowing it to store numerous items while never weighing more than two pounds. The shortest section of the quiver can hold up to sixty arrows or bolts, the middle one contains twelve javelins, and the largest holds six long objects, like quarterstaffs, bows, or spears. Non-archery items of a similar size can sometimes be stored in the appropriate compartment, although they may not always come back out.

GUARDIAN GEAR

Survival is a key component of any successful encounter. Magic items such as the ones on this page are designed to help you not only challenge a powerful foe but also to live to tell the tale of your victory.

DREAD HELM Sometimes your best defense is to look really, really scary. That's where a *dread helm* comes in. This helmet's magic causes your eyes to glow red and hides the rest of your face in shadow, all without affecting your vision. The sharp spikes, sculpted side plates, and angular wings of the helmet add to the imposing effect. While a *dread helm* doesn't technically offer more protection than any other steel helmet, you're a lot less likely to get hit when your opponents are running away in fear.

HELM OF BRILLIANCE Each gem on this helmet is infused with a magic spell: *daylight* for opals, *fireball* for fire opals, *prismatic spray* for diamonds, and *wall of fire* for rubies. Casting a spell causes a gem of that type to disappear from the *helm of brilliance*. When all the gems are gone, the helm loses its magic. So long as the helm has one fire opal, you can command your weapon to burst into flame. If there is at least one diamond, the helm emits a dim light around undead creatures, dealing them additional damage. Avoid fire damage while wearing the helm, since there's a small risk it will activate all the gems at once, injuring everyone nearby and destroying the helm itself.

SCARAB OF PROTECTION

This beetle-shaped medallion might be mistaken for an unusual piece of jewelry, until you hold it in your hand for a few seconds. Then an inscription will appear on its surface that reveals its magical nature. A *scarab of protection* grants its wearer a better chance of resisting spells of all kinds. When affected by necromantic spells or undead powers, adventurers can call upon this amulet to throw off any negative effects. This special ability can be used only twelve times, however, after which the *scarab of protection* crumbles into dust.

SPELLGUARD SHIELD

Shields do a great job of protecting an adventurer from physical attacks. A *spellguard shield* goes a step further by protecting against magical harm as well. Spell attacks are less likely to work thanks to the shield's protective power. It is also easier to resist the effects of all kinds of magic while holding a *spellguard shield*. Such shields are usually decorated with mystical symbols, although that's not always the case.

CURATIVE CONTRAPTIONS

No matter how careful you are, the occasional injury is part of being an adventurer. Whether battling dangerous beasts, traversing rough terrain, tackling magical hazards, or dropping a heavy sack of treasure on your toes, there's plenty of ways to get hurt—or worse—during a quest. The magic items on these pages will help you alleviate the effects of all kinds of harm, from sickness and stubbed toes to death itself.

CAULDRON OF REBIRTH This tiny cast-iron pot is decorated with scenes of heroic adventures and can serve as a spellcasting focus to improve a wizard's or druid's magic. At the end of a long rest, use the cauldron to create a *potion of greater healing* that will last for twenty-four hours. The *cauldron of rebirth* can be increased in size, making it big enough for a medium-size creature to fit inside. Once every seven days, a dead humanoid can be placed inside the cauldron and covered with two hundred pounds of salt. Overnight, the salt will be consumed and the creature returned to life!

KEOGHTOM'S OINTMENT
Developed by a legendary alchemist and explorer, *Keoghtom's ointment* is a thick, gloopy lotion that smells faintly of aloe. It can instantly cure any disease or poisoning and restore the health of the user. The ointment is stored in a glass jar that weighs about half a pound and holds up to five doses.

PERIAPT OF HEALTH
This uncommon amulet features a red stone carved to look like a heart with two faces, one happy and one sad. When wearing a *periapt of health*, it is impossible to contract any disease, either by natural or magical means. If someone is already sick, they will not feel the effects of their illness as long as they are wearing the necklace. This works against all diseases, including those caused by monsters or magic, although it won't help against curses such as lycanthropy.

REINCARNATION DUST
This purple dust inside a small pouch contains powerful but erratic magic. By sprinkling the dust on a dead humanoid—or even just a part of them—the target can be revived! The magic creates an entirely new body for the soul to inhabit. Curiously, this new body is often a different species than the original body. An elf revived by *reincarnation dust* may arise as a dragonborn or a human, for example. However, the dust will not work on anyone who has been dead for more than ten days or anyone who does not want to be revived.

MAGICAL MINDS

While most magic items are straightforward tools, some have a mind of their own. Self-awareness can arise in different ways, including from the magic used to create the item, possession by a supernatural force, or haunting by a previous owner.

Although powerful, such items can be challenging to wield. Sentient magic items have unique personalities, values, quirks, and flaws. Depending on how closely these traits match those of its holder, a sentient magic item may be a cherished ally or a constant threat to the wielder's ideals.

Sentient magic items can communicate, usually by sharing emotions with their holder. Some can speak aloud, and a rare few are telepathic. They can also see and hear their surroundings.

To reflect a sentient item's autonomy, the Dungeon Master (DM) makes decisions about the object's choices. A player may ask the item to use some special power or ability, but the DM decides if the item is willing to cooperate. A sentient item that is angry, offended, or disappointed may withhold its magic or even turn against its wielder. Just like other allies, you'll need to keep up a good relationship with your object.

SPECIAL PURPOSE

Some sentient items have a specific goal or objective. A haunted sword may seek revenge against those who killed its former owner, or a holy axe might only want to fight the undead. Such sentient magic items will cooperate when their wielder works toward a similar aim but become obstinate and unhelpful when their purpose is not respected. A thwarted sentient magic item might even attempt to take control of its wielder, forcing them to act against their will.

BLACKRAZOR

This ghastly greatsword has a dark blade that shines like a star-speckled night sky, and a scabbard decorated with pieces of black stone. The creator's identity has been lost to history, but the wickedness contained within carries on, hungering for souls.

Blackrazor has a forceful personality, speaking inside its wielder's mind with a deep and booming voice. The sword is a bully—angry and insulting. It feels that anyone lucky enough to hold it should obey its commands, not the other way around. The sword believes that everything in the universe came from endless darkness and one day all will return to that same darkness. *Blackrazor*'s purpose is to feed, destroy, and feed again, repeating that process over and over until the end of all things.

SPECIAL PURPOSE Not merely a magic sword, *Blackrazor* is a soul eater. When used to slay an enemy, the sword takes the spirit from their body and uses it as fuel, just like a person eating or drinking to survive. For a short time after *Blackrazor* takes a soul, the wielder gains strength, resilience, and skill in combat—effects that fade unless another soul is claimed.

DO THIS	DON'T DO THIS
Scare your enemies. *Blackrazor*'s reputation as a soul-eating sword is known far and wide. If an enemy recognizes the blade or you tell them of its dark power, they may give up before a fight even starts.	**Don't get overconfident.** The strength that *Blackrazor* gives after feeding is powerful, but only lasts as long as the wielder keeps holding the sword. The moment you let go, that strength is gone.
Feed the blade . . . or else. If *Black-razor* does not consume a soul every three days, it will begin to fight back and look for another wielder more willing to indulge its nasty appetite.	**Don't let yourself be corrupted.** A weapon with such dark power cannot be wielded by those fighting for good. If you must carry this sword as part of a quest, do so carefully.

ORCSPLITTER

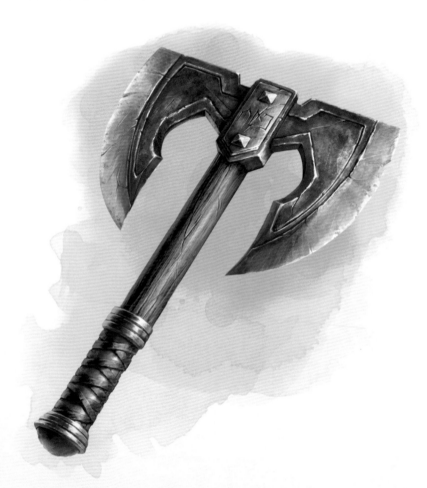

SPECIAL PURPOSE *Orcsplitter* was created to protect dwarves, to serve as a symbol of dwarven resolve and will, and to encourage its holder to defend both individual dwarves and their communities. This greataxe values bravery and loyalty above all, expecting no less from its wielder. Anyone who displays duplicity, deception, or cowardice will struggle to use this weapon effectively. *Orcsplitter* is quite willing to push its champion into danger in its quest to find a more worthy master.

This battered greataxe appears unremarkable on first sight, marked with nicks and scratches from its previous battles. Its only decoration is the dwarven runes for "orc" carved into its head, with a slash that splits the word in half. Yet once, long ago, this very weapon was wielded by dwarven leader Torhild Flametongue as he forged the now-lost kingdom of Besilmer.

Orcsplitter has a grim and inflexible personality, with firm ideas of right and wrong. It yearns to serve a courageous warrior in the pursuit of goodness and justice and will resist attempts to be used for tyranny or oppression. This greataxe mainly communicates by sharing emotions, although at important moments, *Orcsplitter* may seek to guide its wielder with lines from ancient Dwarvish verse.

Designed to oppose the traditional enemies of dwarves—giants, goblins, and, most of all, orcs—the axe silently urges its wielder to face such creatures in combat. Anyone attuned to *Orcsplitter* gains skill in using greataxes, along with an increase in their chances to strike opponents with the weapon. Orcs are especially vulnerable to the axe's magic, and a very lucky blow may even kill one with a single strike. The weapon's courage infuses both its wielder and nearby allies, making the group immune to becoming frightened.

DO THIS	DON'T DO THIS
Learn poetry. Reciting ancient Dwarvish poems will strengthen your bond with *Orcsplitter*, while knowing the stories will give you context for any lines the axe shares with you.	**Don't ignore its warnings.** *Orcsplitter* is neither smart nor charming, but its store of ancient wisdom provides valuable perspective that might just save your life.
Be honest. Too many lies, even small ones, may inspire *Orcsplitter* to break its bond with you.	**Don't use it for mundane tasks.** A weapon that once helped build a mighty kingdom won't tolerate being used to chop firewood.

SNICKER-SNACK

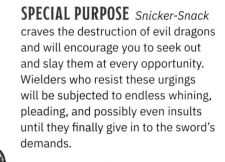

SPECIAL PURPOSE *Snicker-Snack* craves the destruction of evil dragons and will encourage you to seek out and slay them at every opportunity. Wielders who resist these urgings will be subjected to endless whining, pleading, and possibly even insults until they finally give in to the sword's demands.

VORPAL SWORD On a very lucky strike (rolling the highest number on a twenty-sided die), *vorpal swords*, like *Snicker-Snack*, can slice off a creature's head with a single blow. If the creature can't survive without their head, they are instantly killed. This looks very impressive and is a great way to inspire the rest of your opponents to surrender.

However, this power won't activate if the target doesn't have a head, is immune to slashing damage from bladed weapons, or is too large for the blade to cut all the way through their neck, although the blow still does an enormous amount of damage. A creature with multiple heads will only lose one per successful *vorpal sword* strike.

Forged in the fairy realm of the Feywild, *Snicker-Snack* has an unpredictable, chaotic personality that's sure to keep you on your toes. This ornate greatsword is a two-handed weapon that vastly improves the chances of landing a successful blow, even against targets that are normally immune to damage from bladed weapons. With a very lucky blow, this *vorpal sword* might even take an enemy's head clean off!

Snicker-Snack values virtue and honor but often disregards rules, laws, and polite manners. The sword is moderately smart, very insightful, and fantastically charming. *Snicker-Snack* can speak, read, and understand the common language and communicates with a silvery, melodic voice that adds to its appeal.

Once attuned to *Snicker-Snack*, its holder becomes skilled in using greatswords even with no previous melee training. The sword's magic allows the wielder to use charisma instead of physical strength to power blows. However, the weapon's fickle nature means that if the target is missed three times in a row, the sword will end its attunement. To win it back, its wielder will need to take a long rest and then persuade *Snicker-Snack* to give them another chance.

DO THIS	DON'T DO THIS
Be friendly. Sharing jokes and silly stories will make *Snicker-Snack* more likely to forgive you for missed attacks or failing to chase down evil dragons.	**Don't use the blade in minor scuffles.** You won't be able to stop the *vorpal sword* effect if luck strikes, so don't use *Snicker-Snack* against opponents that you aren't willing to risk killing.
Shout the sword's name when you attack. It's not necessary, but it is fun.	

SNICKER-SNACK

Trawli had hoped the blue dragons were a mirage when they first appeared, hallucinations born of too many hours trekking across the arid desert. That hope had vanished when they attacked, clawing the leg of the caravan's lead merchant. She swung her sword in a wide arc, feeling a ripple of power through her arms as Snicker-Snack struck. There was a muted *thunk* as something hit the sand. Trawli stared down in amazement at the dragon head lying lifeless before her. Had she really done that? Taken off a dragon's head with a single blow?

"One down, one to go!" sang Snicker-Snack in a bright, joyous tone. The second blue dragon roared, showing off a spiked jawline that perfectly matched the one near Trawli's feet, and fled. Relief washed over Trawli. There was no way she could be that lucky twice in a row.

"We need to get him to a healer!" shouted her companion, lifting the injured merchant in his arms. The sword's eagerness vibrated through the handle, forcing Trawli to tighten her grip.

"They'll be fine! Hurry up—we can't let that second dragon get away!" Snicker-Snack exclaimed. The dragon had flown east. The nearest healer was at an oasis five miles south. Trawli had to choose a direction, and quickly.

What path should Trawli follow in this situation? If she decides to chase after the dragon, will she manage to catch up with them? Will the rest of her party be able to reach the healer without her protection, or will they face more danger along the way? If she goes south toward the oasis, how will *Snicker-Snack* respond, and what can she do to regain the sword's support? Has the dragon fled for good, or will they return with reinforcements? The story can go in so many directions—the final choice is up to you!

PARTICULAR POTIONS

Potions provide an easy-to-transport, easy-to-use means of accessing a dizzying array of magic effects. Although they can only be used once, a well-timed potion can be a powerful tool in an adventurer's arsenal.

POTION OF ANIMAL FRIENDSHIP If you've ever wanted to pal around with a dangerous critter, this is the potion for you. Drink it down and for the next hour, you'll be able to cast the *animal friendship* spell on one creature of your choosing. The beast must be able to see and hear you, and the spell will instantly break if you or your companions harm the creature. Otherwise, the animal is charmed by you for the next twenty-four hours. The potion works on creatures who walk, fly, swim, and slither, but be warned that very clever critters may be immune to its effects.

POTION OF FIRE BREATH This uncommon potion is sure to ignite fear in your enemies and awe in your allies. After drinking this flickering fluid, you'll be able to breathe a fiery blast at any target within a thirty-foot range (about the length of a school bus). This scorching experience inflicts a lot of damage, on top of being scary and cool. Your fire breath will last for one hour, or until you use it three times. Some potion-users have reported a smoky aftertaste, which can be fixed with a good teeth-brushing.

POTION OF GIANT STRENGTH Prepare for a mighty flex once you guzzle this magic potion. For one hour after drinking, you'll have the same strength as a giant, packed into your regular-size body. You can use that strength to do all kinds of things, like lift heavy objects, fight powerful monsters, or beat all your friends at arm wrestling.

Just like giants, this potion comes in six varieties, with strength and rarity changing based on the giant type. Hill giant potions give the smallest gain, followed by frost, stone, fire, and cloud giants. Storm giant potions are powerful and rare enough to be considered legendary. That makes sense when you realize that every *potion of giant strength* requires a special ingredient—a fingernail sliver from the relevant giant type. Yum!

POTION OF HEROISM Sometimes even the bravest adventurers need a little supplemental support when faced with a daunting challenge. That's where a *potion of heroism* can help. Imbibing this elixir provides a temporary boost of perseverance, letting the drinker withstand a little extra damage for the next hour. In addition, they'll gain the effects of the *bless* spell, giving a bonus when attacking enemies and resisting their assaults.

POTENT PROSTHETICS

In a world where denizens range in size from halfling-small to giant-tall and may have tails, horns, scales, fur, or tortoise shells, physical differences are an expected part of life. Some adventurers don't feel the need for assistive devices, like legendary cleric Bel Vala, who embraces her blindness. Others use magic items to offset their disabilities—or in some cases, to give them greatly enhanced abilities!

ARCANE PROPULSION ARM Designed by artificers (see page 69) of Eberron, this item can only be used by those individuals missing a hand or an arm. Once attuned to the wearer, the magic creates a copy of the missing limb. It functions as a prosthetic and cannot be removed against the wielder's will. An *arcane propulsion arm* doubles as a magic melee weapon capable of hitting targets with force damage similar to the *magic missile* spell. The prosthetic can also be used as a thrown weapon that can attack at range. After striking a target, an *arcane propulsion arm* immediately returns and reattaches to its wielder.

ERSTAZ EYE This artificial eye replaces a real one that was lost or removed. Once in place, it can't be removed by anyone else. The wielder can see through the tiny orb as if it were a normal eyeball for their species. An *ersatz eye* is often enchanted to match the color and appearance of an existing eye, although some users prefer a mismatched look.

PROSTHETIC LIMB A prosthetic limb is designed to replace a missing body part, such as a hand, foot, arm, or leg. They can be made from a variety of materials, although wood or metal are the most common, and may be of simple or ornate design. A magic *prosthetic limb* functions identically to the part it replaces. The user can attach or detach it easily, but it cannot be removed against their will. A *prosthetic limb* does not require attunement, so it does not count toward limitations on the number of attuned magic items a character may have.

INFUSED INSTRUMENTS

The idea that music is magic takes concrete shape through the enchanted instruments on these pages. Most can only be attuned by bards, although some instruments—like the *pipes of haunting*—can be played by anyone who possesses the right skills.

INSTRUMENT OF THE BARDS There are seven different types of these extraordinary instruments: the cittore, bandore, lute, lyre, mandolin, and two different types of harp. When played, the attuned musician can choose to cast one of seven different spells bound to the instrument. Four spells—*fly, invisibility, levitate,* and *protection from good and evil*—are common to all, while the other three spells vary depending on the instrument. The rarest instrument is the *Ollamh harp*, a legendary object capable of controlling the weather and summoning a fire storm.

LYRE OF BUILDING This small, U-shaped, stringed instrument lets you heal physical objects. While holding the lyre, you can cast the *mending* spell to repair a break or tear in any item that you touch. When a nearby object or building is damaged, you can also play it to temporarily protect the structure. Once per day, the *lyre of building* allows you to cast one of four different spells to do things such as create passages in walls, move large amounts of dirt, create finished objects from raw materials, and summon an enchanted construct.

PIPES OF HAUNTING

Carved from bone and decorated with animal skulls, these creepy windpipes sound just as scary as they look. By expending a charge, the musician can play an eerie tune that frightens all nearby listeners. Creatures who succumb to the magic music find it harder to attack or approach the musician for one minute. You must know how to play wind instruments to use the *pipes of haunting*. An untrained player can create a dreadful sound with them, but it won't have the magic effect!

REVELER'S CONCERTINA

This squeezebox-style instrument is similar to an accordion, although smaller and lighter, and produces a bright, upbeat sound. Just holding a *reveler's concertina* makes all your bardic spells a little more effective. While playing the concertina, you can cast the instrument's special spell—*Otto's irresistible dance*—against one nearby creature. The target immediately begins a comical dance that lasts for one minute, during which they are less able to attack or defend themselves. They also look very, very silly. The concertina can only create this effect once a day.

SNEAKY SUPPLIES

Stealth may be a rogue specialty, but any character can benefit from these magic items designed to help you access locked places, travel unseen, and move heavy items with relative ease.

CHIME OF OPENING The clear tone that this hollow metal tube makes when struck is capable of opening objects that would otherwise resist imposing physical force or the most skilled lockpicks. One lock or latch on the selected object opens with each note sounded, provided that the chime's sound can reach the object. If no locks or latches remain, the object itself opens. After sounding ten times, the chimes crack and become useless.

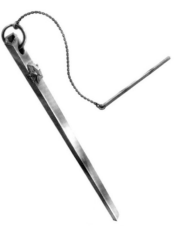

DUST OF DISAPPEARANCE This magic powder has the look and feel of very fine beach sand. When thrown into the air, all creatures and objects within ten feet become invisible. They cannot be seen, except by other creatures using magic or possessing extraordinary senses. However, those invisible will still make noise and leave tracks that might give away their location. The effect lasts for two to eight minutes, but can be broken if the user attacks or casts a spell. Unfortunately, the *dust of disappearance* doesn't reappear, which means each packet can only be used once.

IMMOVABLE ROD Imagine how useful it would be to defy gravity whenever you wanted. That's the magic of the *immovable rod*, which becomes stationary when the button on one end is pressed. No matter where you are when the button is pressed—falling through the sky, scaling an icy cliff, jumping over a sleeping dragon's horde—the rod locks into place. Incredibly strong creatures might be able to move the rod a few feet with extreme effort, and loading the rod with more than eight thousand pounds will cause it to deactivate.

PORTABLE HOLE Carrying an extradimensional hole in your pocket can be surprisingly useful. This fine black cloth starts about the size of a handkerchief but unfolds into a six-foot round sheet that, when placed against a solid surface, opens up into a ten-foot-deep hole. You can fill the hole with almost anything that fits and close it back up by folding in the edges. Since everything inside is being stored in another dimension, the *portable hole* remains practically weightless.

There's only ten minutes of breathable air in the hole, so don't store living creatures inside for longer or they might suffocate! Trapped creatures can try to break out, reappearing within five feet of the hole's location if they succeed. It's a terrible idea to place one extradimensional container, like a *bag of holding* or a *portable hole*, inside a different one. The resulting blast will destroy both items and toss everyone nearby through a magic portal that promptly vanishes forever.

TREMENDOUS TOMES

Some adventurers believe that all books contain a little magic. With the tomes described here, there can be no doubt! Many magic books can only be used by wizards, who are trained to bring forth spells from written pages, although some tomes are accessible to everyone.

ATLAS OF ENDLESS HORIZONS Bound in dark leather, this thick book is crisscrossed with inlaid silver lines resembling a map or a chart. That's no coincidence, because this atlas contains a variety of spells capable of moving the user from place to place, or even between dimensions or planes of existence. The book has three charges (see page 87) and regains some used charges each dawn. The charges allow you to replace one of your memorized spells with a different spell from the book, or to teleport up to ten feet when hit by an attack.

FULMINATING TREATISE This thick spellbook reeks of smoke and ozone, with sparks of energy cracking along the edges of its scorched pages. It contains seven spells—among them, *fireball*, *gust of wind*, *magic missile*, and *thunderwave*. The book has three charges and gains back some used charges each dawn. The charges allow you to replace one of your memorized spells with a different spell from the book, or to do additional damage to a creature who has already been injured by one of your spells.

MANUAL OF BODILY HEALTH This book contains detailed information on health and nutrition, written on magic-infused pages. By studying the *manual of bodily health* and following its advice for forty-eight hours over a six-day period, you will significantly improve your physical endurance. Similar manuals exist for increasing your dexterity (*manual of quickness of action*) and your strength (*manual of gainful exercise*). Magic manuals require one century to regain their power after being used.

TOME OF UNDERSTANDING This magic volume is filled with exercises to improve your intuition and insight. If you spend forty-eight hours during a six-day period reading the *tome of understanding* and practicing the exercises, you'll notice a decided increase in your wisdom. Related references exist for improving your charisma (*tome of leadership and influence*) and your intelligence (*tome of clear thought*). These magic books require one century to regain their power after being used.

USEFUL ODDITIES

Sometimes adventurers come across magic items that are so unusual it seems remarkable that anyone dreamt them up in the first place. These quirky creations often prove to be surprisingly useful, especially when you apply a little imagination to exploring their possibilities.

ABRACADABRUS This ornate wooden chest is studded all over with gemstones, with enough space inside to fit an average beach ball. To use, touch the closed lid and name an inexpensive, nonmagical object, which magically appears inside the *abracadabrus*. Conjured food is delicious and nourishing, but spoils after twenty-four hours. Gems and precious metals vanish after one minute. An *abracadabrus* has up to twenty charges, recovering a random number each dawn. If the chest runs out of charges, its gemstones might turn to dust, ending its magic forever.

BAG OF BEANS This heavy bag contains between four and twelve dried beans. If you plant a single bean in the ground and water it, a random magic effect pops up one minute later. Possibilities include a blue campfire, pink toads that turn into monsters, a giant beanstalk, or a sixty-foot pyramid with a mummy lord inside. If you dump all the bag's contents on the ground at once, the beans produce an explosion that damages everything within ten feet and ignites all flammable objects.

DAERN'S INSTANT FORTRESS

Most adventurers make do with open campfires or simple tents when sleeping out in the wild. The ones lucky enough to possess this wondrous and rare magic item can, instead, take shelter in their very own fortress. With a command word, this one-inch metal cube expands into a square tower twenty feet wide and thirty feet high. Inside the fortress are two floors connected by a ladder. There are arrow slits on all the walls and a magic door that opens only at your command. Creatures in the way will be pushed aside as the building expands, sometimes being injured in the process. A second command word collapses *Daern's instant fortress* back into a metal cube, provided the tower is empty.

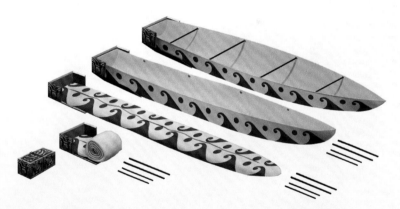

FOLDING BOAT

This handy item is a welcome addition to any expedition party that travels over both land and water. In its basic form the *folding boat* appears as a rectangular wooden box about one foot long and weighing four pounds. Three different command words activate its magic properties. The first causes the box to unfold into a ten-foot boat capable of carrying four medium creatures. The second command produces a larger vessel with room for fifteen creatures. The final word collapses the *folding boat* back into its box form. This only works if no living creatures are inside the vessel, so you won't get dumped in the water if you accidentally say the command word while sailing.

PECULIAR PHENOMENA

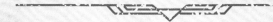

Manju, Shana, and Fen came to the apple orchard looking for magic—but found more enchantment than they'd expected. As they ran for their lives, apples tumbling from their arms, they understood why the bard they met on the road had laughed when he told them about the old orchard. A colony of mimics had taken over, disguising themselves as bushels, baskets, carts, cart wheels, and apple presses. These devious creatures were using the magic of the apples to lure unwary travelers to their doom.

From healing properties in unusual fruit to hungry monsters hiding in plain sight, magic can sometimes be found in unexpected places. Lingering magic from wars long ago may transform a quiet garden. A warlock's ambitious spellcasting may get tangled in a raging storm. Intrusions from another world may steer a familiar road in an unfamiliar direction.

Here you'll learn about some of the unexpected phenomena you might encounter on the road. Watch your step as you venture forward. You can never be sure what astonishing circumstance you're wandering into!

ELDRITCH STORMS

DO THIS

Watch the sky. Eldritch storms can happen fast, but there can be warning signs.

Seek shelter. Just be sure that your shelter is strong enough to survive this type of storm.

DON'T DO THIS

Don't keep going. These storms are almost impossible to pass through.

Don't ignore the consequences. The storm is not the only thing to worry about. You may also have to deal with wildfires or a zombie attack.

On their own, both magic and weather can be wild, unpredictable, and terrifyingly powerful. Imagine the possibilities when those forces come together. Sometimes powerful magic gets caught up on the winds, creating what is known as an eldritch storm. These storms may seep through from otherworldly planes where the elements are raw and powerful, or they may be the result of bad weather over cursed or enchanted land. Some may even be the deliberate creations of a spellcaster—perhaps as a weapon of war or a way to keep visitors away from a specific place.

FLAME STORM If you see dark thunderclouds rippling with intense red light, beware! Flame storms' deafening thunder and jagged lightning can be devastating, but it's the fire rain that you really need to worry about. The fiery droplets set alight any flammable materials on which they land. Flame storms usually last only a few minutes, but once elemental magic has become entangled in an ordinary storm, multiple flame storms may follow.

FLAYWIND Originating in extradimensional planes of desolation and madness, flaywinds are sandstorms so intense that they can strip a body down to the bones. A flaywind can manifest in seconds, creating a wall of grit and debris that is impossible to see through and almost impossible to pass through. The only sure way to survive a flaywind is to avoid it completely. If you do get caught in one, only the sturdiest of shelters will offer any protection.

NECROTIC TEMPEST Death magic unfurls and twists through the dark clouds of a necrotic tempest, creating haunting apparitions of screaming skulls and skeletal figures in the sky. Any living creature touched by a necrotic tempest may be killed in an instant, and even survivors will find that their skin begins to rot on their bones. Those who do not survive become zombies or animated skeletons, so a necrotic tempest over a densely populated area can create an army of the undead.

THRYM'S HOWL Named for the legendary god of the frost giants, Thrym's Howl is a blinding blizzard that freezes the ground it touches and most living things caught in its fury. The howl descends like a wall of snow, obliterating sight and sound for as long as a day. Even adventurers built for the cold will find the blizzard impossible to pass through. For anyone else, this icy storm may mark the end of their journey.

EMOTIONAL ECHOES

DO THIS

Speak to locals. Residents may be able to warn you if there's an emotional echo nearby.

Keep calm. The most levelheaded members of an adventuring party are least likely to be affected.

DON'T DO THIS

Don't hold a grudge. Travelers can say or do things after passing through an emotional echo that they may later come to regret.

Don't linger. If you stay too long in an emotional echo, you may be forever changed by your actions.

Magic is not always loud, bright, or explosive. It can touch the world in subtle ways as well. Emotional echoes are one of these subtle forms of magic—places where a single powerful emotion has changed the nature of a location. They aren't created by design but by accident. When powerful joy or tragedy reshapes the environment, the feelings from that distant time can "echo" in the present. Sometimes a single event creates this emotional resonance, such as a great victory on a tournament ground. Other times it can build up over years, such as the despair that haunts a sinister schoolhouse. An echo may claim a single room or building, or it may infuse an entire lake or a forest. The echo works like a *suggestion* spell. Anyone within range may become overwhelmed and act based on that strong emotion. Even after departing the echo's zone, the effects can linger for up to a day.

EXAMPLES OF EMOTIONAL ECHOES INCLUDE:

CAVERN OF FEAR
It's natural to be afraid of the dark, but in an underground passage where fear has seeped into the walls, an adventurer's own deepest fears can come bubbling to the surface.

FIELD OF VALOR
Where once a battle was fought between two valiant armies, now only a quiet meadow remains— but those passing through may be compelled to undertake acts of sudden and possibly foolish bravery.

LOVERS' LANE
A secret lane where lovers used to meet, now overgrown with flowers and wild vines, can become a place where travelers suddenly confess their secret loves to each other.

PIT OF RAGE
The site of an old tavern that hosted bare-knuckle brawls over many centuries is now just a clearing in the woods, but those who enter that space as friends may quickly turn on one another.

VISTA OF INSPIRATION
A clifftop view that inspired a great work of art may find itself layering echo on echo as others feel that same surge of inspiration and produce great works of their own—so long as the view remains undisturbed.

ENCHANTED SPRINGS

GUARDIANS OF THE SPRINGS

Guardians take many forms, including faithful followers of the entity that blessed the spring or a powerful creature aligned to that entity. Sometimes it is the entity itself. Examples of guardians include dragons, unicorns, golems, giants, snakes, and sphinxes.

Some guardians will attack anyone who approaches their spring, while others will test visitors to see if they are worthy. Some guardians permit only certain types of adventurers to pass, such as a faithful paladin or a purehearted child. Guardians also decide who can take enchanted water away with them. Anyone trying to steal water without the guardian's blessing may discover that its magical effects have faded away.

Natural springs are cherished spots offering clean, fresh water. Sometimes, powerful entities make them even more special by blessing these springs with magical properties. Drinking or bathing in these enchanted waters can grant a visitor the benefits of its magic—and occasionally the explorer can take the magic with them in an enchanted flask or bottle. However, many springs are protected by a guardian, who decides whether someone can or cannot reach the water.

Healing water is the most sought-after type of enchanted spring, but that's far from the only magic effect found in these waters. An enchanted spring could give you a coat of glowing protective feathers, the wall-crawling ability of a spider, or a third eye on your forehead that can spy things hidden by magic. Other springs may grant you a singing voice that captivates all listeners, eyestalks so you can see in all directions, or donkey ears that let you hear for great distances. Sometimes the effects have no clear benefit, such as making you grow a tail or a crown of flowers. Whatever the effect, an enchanted spring's magic usually fades after a few days.

CURSED SPRINGS

Unwary travelers may find themselves in greater danger after drinking or touching a corrupted spring. Other adventurers may seek out these dark waters for their own wicked ends. Cursed springs might drain the victim's health, cause their flesh to slowly decay, or even turn them into a werewolf.

DO THIS	DON'T DO THIS
Pay attention. Even if you can't see a guardian, they may see you.	**Don't steal.** Even if you succeed, the magic may not work.
Remember the price. This magic often carries side effects, so be prepared.	**Don't ignore clues.** The pathway to a spring can be marked with warning signs—or the remains of previous visitors.

ENCHANTED SPRINGS

Florizan and his friend Kalista had been attacked by bandits on the road and barely managed to escape with their lives. The arrow wound in Florizan's shoulder was easily bandaged, but Kalista was more seriously hurt. The young bard knew that she'd need healing magic to fully recover.

Florizan had heard stories of an enchanted spring in the caverns beneath Longsaddle, so he carried Kalista here in the hope that the guardian of the spring would grant them favor. Kalista was in no condition to climb down the rope ladder that led to the water, so Florizan ventured in alone, leaving her at the mouth of the cave.

This enchanted spring was rumored to be protected by a stone golem, but there was no sign of any such guardian nearby. Even worse, the water's surface had a slick black appearance that Florizan found disturbing. Could he be sure that he was in the right place? What would happen if this water was cursed rather than blessed?

Should Florizan test the water's effects on his own injury before attempting to heal Kalista? Should he seek out the golem to receive a blessing, or take the water to the mouth of the cave and risk the guardian's wrath? The choice is yours to make!

MIMIC COLONIES

ADOPTING A MIMIC

An overpowered mimic colony may be willing to surrender one of its offspring to an interested adventurer. These juvenile mimics inherit the colony's ability to communicate, providing the rare opportunity to train that mimic as a companion creature. A shapeshifting monster who eats your enemies is a good friend to have, so long as you're sure you share a strong bond.

Mimics are shapeshifting creatures that attempt to devour adventurers by taking the shape of intriguing or ordinary objects—such as a treasure chest or a chair—to lure them in. Mimics are usually solitary predators, but occasionally a group will establish a colony. Joining together like this allows them to create a much bigger trap, one that can be even harder to detect.

Mimic colonies might appear to be a tavern, an oasis, or even a whole village. A band of unwary travelers wandering into a colony may suddenly find themselves surrounded by terrible teeth and grasping tendrils, or even covered in burning acid spewed from the mimics' mouths. Adventurers stopping in a beautiful glade for lunch may discover that they *are* the lunch.

Mimic colonies are smarter than individual mimics. They share a telepathic bond and can communicate with other creatures, including you. If you can outwit or overpower a mimic colony, they may be willing to negotiate for their survival.

DO THIS	DON'T DO THIS
Be suspicious. If you come across something too good to be true on your travels, be on your guard.	**Don't brawl.** Mimics secrete a sticky substance that allows them to cling to their prey, so keep your distance.
Look for citizens. Mimic colonies are often suspiciously empty because the mimics can't resist eating all the visitors.	**Don't rely on your surroundings.** Grabbing a chair to fight a mimic won't help if the chair is also a mimic—one that's now trying to eat your hand!

PRIMAL FRUIT

IDENTIFYING PRIMAL FRUIT

Trees and plants that bear primal fruit will also bear large amounts of ordinary fruit, but the primal fruit is usually easy to identify. It may have an exceptionally vibrant color, glittering skin, or an unnatural glow. It may even produce ethereal music or feel strange to the touch.

The natural world has a power all its own, known as primal magic. Adventurers who know the signs can attempt to find and harness that power. Primal fruit is one example of this phenomenon.

Eating primal fruit can produce remarkable results—and equally powerful side effects. Primal fruit carries its power for about a week, even when harvested, cooked, or juiced. Some magic-users have been able to grow primal fruit in gardens, groves, and orchards. More often, it grows naturally in places touched by powerful magic, like wild forests or sacred groves.

POSSIBLE EFFECTS AND SIDE EFFECTS

Primal magic shares the untamed quality of the natural world where it is found, providing both benefits and strange side effects.

The fruit provides a burst of strength for one hour, then leaves you exhausted.

The fruit makes you resistant to sword attacks for an hour, but your skin constantly feels prickly.

The fruit protects you against death for several hours but leaves you feeling like you've been poisoned.

The fruit makes you resistant to spells but damages your senses.

The fruit lets you survive without food, drink, or sleep for several days but afflicts you with visions.

The fruit lets you communicate telepathically but fills your mind with whispers that are difficult to ignore.

The fruit heals you but causes your skin to glow for an hour.

DO THIS

Try to identify the magic. Some spells can reveal the properties of a piece of primal fruit, though not always the side effects.

Make juice. Turning the primal fruit into other types of food can make it easier to keep and easier to hide.

DON'T DO THIS

Don't all eat together. Because of the side effects, it's a good idea if only one member of the adventuring party eats the primal fruit at a time.

Don't get greedy. No one knows for sure what the side effects might be from too much primal fruit.

UNEARTHLY ROADS

ACCESSING AN UNEARTHLY ROAD

The entrance to an unearthly road is sometimes marked with an archway or milestone that reveals its supernatural nature. In other cases, the path may be blocked by an obstacle, like fallen rocks or a sleeping giant. Some may look perfectly ordinary.

Once you've identified an unearthly road, you may need a key to unlock it. You might need to hold a specific magic item or wear a special garment. Maybe you need to make a sacrifice or make a deal with a spirit that guards the way. Unearthly roads are like tunnels: you enter at one end and exit at the other, but it is very difficult to leave partway through the journey.

There are some roads that will never appear on an ordinary map, routes that connect two places by methods other than simple geography. These unearthly roads bend the usual rules of space and time to take travelers to faraway lands or even other realms.

Sometimes these supernatural paths remain stable for years, even generations, allowing the creation of trade routes between lands that may not have discovered each other through ordinary means. Other routes may be stable but secret, serving as a way for a powerful spellcaster to gather resources from an otherwise unreachable mountain peak, or for a cruel warlord to transport an army without anyone knowing his plans.

Some unearthly roads are unstable. They may only open at a certain time, such as under a full moon or once every hundred years. They may shift locations, so that a course that once led to a famous library now ends on an island full of dinosaurs. Choosing to journey along an unearthly road requires bravery, research, and a dash of luck.

DO THIS

Prepare. Make sure you have everything you'll need at both the entrance and the exit of the unearthly road, especially if one end is a frozen wasteland and the other is a desert.

Stay together. If the members of your adventuring party do not enter and exit the road together, you may find yourselves arriving in different places.

DON'T DO THIS

Don't lose track. Remember the location of the exit from which you emerge if you plan on making a return journey.

Don't let down your guard. You may not be the only travelers on an unearthly road. There might be complications and dangers on the road itself.

CURIOUS CONSTRUCTS

The adventuring party was not merely lost, they were trapped with no hope of escape. The artificer known as Dwallum had offered to provide them with weapons to protect their village from a young dragon that destroyed their neighbors. They only had to reach Dwallum at his forge, somewhere deep in the mines beneath the fortress of Ironslag—and bring him a gift from his daughter.

Somehow, the party had found themselves stuck in a room with no doors—a magical trap for unwary visitors. They feared they would never escape. Then they heard the *clang, clang, clang* of approaching footsteps. Heavy steps. Very heavy steps.

When the iron golem crashed through the wall, the adventurers immediately attacked in a desperate bid to survive. How could they have known that Dwallum himself had sent the golem to their rescue?

Constructs are unlike any other beings you might encounter on an adventure. Made from lifeless materials, they are animated by magic and infused with spirits that allow them to move and communicate. Often tough, strong, and possessing unusual immunities, constructs can be significant obstacles—or useful allies.

DANGER LEVELS

Each construct profile includes a number indicating the danger level of that creation, with a **0** being harmless, a **1** as a reasonable threat for a beginner adventurer, and building up from there. A **5** is incredibly dangerous and requires an experienced group of adventurers to possibly defeat it.

CONSTRUCTS OVERVIEW

In worlds dominated by magic, filled with entities such as unicorns, dragons, and giants, there are some who say constructs are the most disconcerting creatures that they have ever encountered— if they would call them "creatures" at all. Constructs are artificial beings made of inorganic or dead materials, like stone, clay, wood, or metal. Though they are created using magic, constructs require crafting expertise and engineering skills, making them products of science as much as magic. This fact can make them seem strange even to adventurers who are used to dealing with fey, lycanthropes, or the undead.

Artificers (see page 69) are experts when it comes to creating constructs—their technical approach to magic gives them all the skills they need to build and animate anything from a small clockwork assistant to an imposing stone defender.

FUNCTIONS

Constructs are always created to serve a purpose, and most of them fall into one of three categories.

Helpers: Constructs designed to assist their creator or act as a servant or companion. This includes the homunculi favored by artificers, and golems created by high priests.

Protectors: Constructs that guard locations, conduct patrols, or act as bodyguards to their creators. Many clockwork creations fall into this category. Golems can also perform this role.

Warriors: Constructs can be built to be very strong and very tough, and they follow orders without question, making them incredibly effective soldiers. The warforged are the most famous example of this type.

IMMUNITIES

Because constructs are inorganic, they are immune to certain conditions that affect organic life. They cannot be poisoned and do not require food, drink, air, or sleep. They are unaffected by psychic attacks and cannot be charmed or frightened. Constructs do not need to rely on ordinary senses.

CREATING CONSTRUCTS

Constructs are not easy to make, and that's just as well. If they were, all the worlds might be overrun with armies of constructs doing the bidding of wealthy elites, plunging the land into endless war—which is exactly what happened with the warforged of Eberron (see page 64).

Most constructs are created by spellcasting, which requires expertise and knowledge of a specific type of *summoning* spell. The effect is often temporary.

Golems are different, as they are built to last a very long time. They can only be made with the help of a book called a *manual of golems*. Using these books exacts a high price on the creator, however, and requires an authoritative knowledge of magic.

SUMMONING A CONSTRUCT

To use a *summoning* spell, the summoner chooses a material such as clay, metal, or stone, then gives it the desired form and calls upon an elemental spirit to inhabit the material. The resulting creation is loyal to the summoner and will obey all their commands as far as it is able.

Different materials come with different benefits and limitations. Metal constructs are well armored, but dangerously hot to the touch. Stone constructs are heavy and dense, but move slowly. Clay constructs are the least protected but the most malleable, and they can use their clay form to lash out at attackers.

Constructs cannot be poisoned or fatigued, and usually cannot be charmed or paralyzed. They will last only as long as the effects of the spell that created them—or until they are destroyed by other means.

MANUAL OF GOLEMS

These rare books provide an extensive guide to all the techniques and materials required to build one type of golem, which are typically made from metal, stone, or clay. But some manuals offer instructions on using unusual materials such as snow or even humanoid flesh. The manuals are unreadable to most adventurers. Only those with the appropriate magical training can decipher the words. Anyone else will experience terrible pain every time they look at the pages.

Creating a golem is expensive and time-consuming. The process costs thousands of gold pieces and requires months of dedicated study. When the process is almost complete, the manual will burst into flames, and its ashes are used to bring the golem to life. Therefore each book can be used only once.

GOLEMS

Golems are crafted from humble materials but possess incredible power and durability. These mindless servants have no independent thoughts and feel no pain, existing only to obey their creator's commands.

CLAY GOLEM Built by high priests who trap spirits in clay bodies, these golems are obedient servants and protectors of sacred sites. Some are beautifully carved by master artisans, while others are more roughly put together in forms only vaguely reminiscent of humans. Clay is not a strong vessel, so if the golem's form is seriously damaged, the spirit may escape, leaving the body to attack everyone around it indiscriminately. The golem must be destroyed or repaired to end its rampage.

Clay golems often outlive their creators, continuing to attend to their duties without thought or desire. If the creator used an amulet as a focus to control the golem, another adventurer can take over command by acquiring the amulet.

FLESH GOLEM The most disgusting form of golem, these constructs are built out of humanoid body parts stitched and bolted together. Flesh golems are enchanted with many of the same immunities as other constructs, but they are afraid of fire. A blast of lightning, however, can return them to full strength.

IRON GOLEM

Larger and tougher than all other types of golems, iron golems have bodies constructed of wrought metal, usually shaped to resemble armor. Strong and heavy, they can crush enemies with a single punch or slice them in two with one swing of a sword. They can also vomit forth clouds of poisonous gas. Iron golems are almost unstoppable. Only magic items or weapons forged from a rare metal called adamantine stand a chance of doing any damage to their towering form.

SNOW GOLEM

Like other types of golems, snow golems are elemental spirits trapped inside physical bodies, but in their case the bodies are made of snow. This provides excellent camouflage in snowy terrain, and most weapons pass harmlessly through them. However, snow golems are very vulnerable to fire.

STONE GOLEM

Stone golems are much tougher than clay golems as they are carved from single blocks of dense, heavy stone. Often, they are carved in humanoid forms, but they can also be given beastly shapes, such as griffins, sphinxes, or lions. Stone golems are impervious to most forms of attack by magic or weapons, and they are surrounded by a time-distorting effect that can disorient and slow down attackers.

CLOCKWORKS

Clockwork constructs are complicated creations with impressive defensive and offensive abilities. The engineering skills of an experienced artificer are required to create one. Multiple copies of some constructs exist, like the gnomish bronze scouts. Others are so ambitious and elaborate that there may only ever be one of them, like the terrifying clockwork kraken.

BRONZE SCOUT Bronze scouts are built by gnomes to protect and defend their underground homes. Resembling giant centipedes, these creatures are capable of vicious attacks thanks to their sharp beaks, multiple blades, and ability to emit an electrical shock. Usually, they patrol the underground boundaries of gnomish territories, listening to the vibrations of creatures on the surface and occasionally extending their stalk-like eyes above the surface when they sense unusual activity.

The scouts can use their electrical powers to send a warning pulse to nearby gnomes before surging to the surface to attack. Like other constructs, they do not require food, water, or even air or sleep, which makes them excellent guards. Unfortunately for the gnomes, these creatures are very expensive to make, requiring huge amounts of bronze and gemstones.

CLOCKWORK KRAKEN The Clockwork Kraken is the unique and peculiar protector of an isolated and almost abandoned city. Rather than a single clockwork entity, the kraken consists of eight tentacles that move independently of each other. These tentacles use their flight and teleportation abilities to patrol the city, attacking any intruders they find. The only way to defeat the tentacles is to locate the engine of the kraken, which is kept in a secret location. The spirit that powers this monstrosity belongs to a kenku high priest whose remains are stored in the engine like a coffin. Only by cracking the engine open and removing the priest's remains can the kraken be deactivated.

STONE DEFENDER Stone defenders make excellent sentries for anyone with a fortress to protect. With the right spells in place, these constructs can stand motionless for years, decades, even centuries. They can camouflage themselves behind the giant stone slabs on their arms, making them virtually undetectable.

When alerted to intruders, they use those stone slabs to block attacks and to protect and defend the entrance. Their large, heavy stone bodies are resistant to most forms of attack. The stone slabs can also be used to strike back, and there aren't many adventurers who will get back up after being hit full force by these rocks.

CLOCKWORKS

The orcish druid named Dawan Pax had traveled across many lands seeking to protect animals that are being hunted for sport. His latest journey brought him to Chult, where a group of wealthy merchants planned to hunt dinosaurs for their own entertainment. Now Dawan Pax was hunting *them*.

As he approached the hunters' camp, Dawan was surprised by a giant insectoid creature surging out of the ground. Impossible! How could any creature sneak up on him without him sensing its life force? As Dawan wrestled to stop the beast from slashing him with its scythe-like appendages and braced against its electrical attacks, he realized that this was not a living creature at all. It was a clockwork construct. Such creations were not native to this land. The hunters must have brought it as protection.

Dawan Pax was unsure what to make of the clockwork machine. Was this a mockery of the gift of life, which he cherished in all creatures? Or was this also a creature of a kind, forced to serve cruel masters?

What would you do? Do you think the construct is a living creature, or is it just a machine? Would you try to destroy it, or try to save it? Will you still be able to stop the hunters while they're under the clockwork's protection? It's your decision to make!

HOUSEHOLD CONSTRUCTS

Not all constructs are created for travel or combat. Some find a place in the home, often in a protective capacity. Such constructs are easily mistaken for ordinary household items until they are activated by the touch or presence of an unfamiliar visitor.

BROOM OF ANIMATED ATTACK This household construct looks exactly like a normal broom until touched, at which point it activates and attempts to escape from being held. If successful, the broom immediately attacks whoever touched it, flying around them while whacking and thwapping their target with both bristles and handle. Some brooms of animated attack can be ridden as if they were a *broom of flying*, but only by their creators.

GUARDIAN PORTRAIT Have you ever felt like a painting was watching you? If the picture was a guardian portrait, it probably was! These constructs feature a realistic image of a specific person, often someone famous, with magic bound into the canvas and frame. Normally motionless, the image becomes animated when the portrait strikes. A guardian portrait can't make physical attacks, but it can cast spells that charm opponents, create visual hallucinations, move objects with telekinesis, and block the spellcasting of others.

RUG OF SMOTHERING Few things are quite so humbling as disarming a series of nasty traps and taking out watchful guards, only to be stopped by the very carpet beneath your feet. This construct can have many forms—from an ornately woven wool rug to a simple reed mat—but all rugs of smothering work the same way. When stepped on by an intruder, the rug springs to life, wrapping tight around its target and smothering them to death. An adventurer's allies will need to be careful while trying to free the victim from this bind, since half the damage done to the rug will actually be inflicted on the trapped person instead.

SKITTERWIDGET These surprisingly cute constructs resemble oversized metal cockroaches with dogs' heads, and speak a language made of high-pitched squeals. They are bound to a magical control ring, which allows the wielder to command up to seven of the constructs at once. They're mostly used for tasks such as cleaning, fetching tools, or delivering messages, although they can also be left to guard locations. Skitterwidgets can mate and breed, producing adorable offspring called kiddywidgets. They are dedicated parents, and even unrelated skitterwidgets will do their best to protect any nearby kiddywidgets.

SHIELD GUARDIAN

SHIELD GUARDIAN AMULET

Every shield guardian is linked to a single magic amulet, and their sole focus is to protect the amulet's wearer. This amulet is a four-inch-wide disk composed of silver-framed wood, with a rune carved into its face. If the amulet is destroyed, the shield guardian is incapacitated until a replacement is made. However, the amulet can only be damaged when it is not being worn or held. Anyone attuned to the amulet gains control over the shield guardian. Wealthy nobles (and scoundrels) are often willing to pay large sums for such a treasure.

These intimidating constructs are created by wizards and other spellcasters to provide protection. They do not require air, food, drink, or sleep, making them ideal sentinels capable of standing guard around the clock. Controlled by a shield guardian amulet, these constructs can be ordered to attack the amulet keeper's opponents if needed. Their primary function is defense, however. They are capable of magically absorbing damage done to the amulet keeper, even at a distance. They are also self-repairing, slowly patching themselves back together as a fight goes on.

Spellcasters can make special use of a shield guardian by storing a single spell within the construct. This spell can be unleashed at any point, by use of a command word or preestablished condition, such as the spellcaster being knocked unconscious.

LAIR Shield guardians usually remain close to their keeper, living in the same space as whoever wears their amulet. A shield guardian always knows the distance and direction to their amulet and can be telepathically summoned by the amulet's wearer at any time.

SIZE Made mostly of metal with some wooden sections, shield guardians vary in height from eight to sixteen feet, or about the size of two refrigerators stacked atop each other.

DO THIS	DON'T DO THIS
Look for hidden constructs. If your attacks are doing less damage against a spellcaster than you'd expect, they may have a concealed shield guardian nearby.	**Don't give it time to repair.** Remember that a shield guardian is self-repairing, so take it down as fast as you can.
Beware its stored spell. You never know what magic a shield guardian could contain or what will release its spell.	**Don't ignore the amulet.** If you can separate the amulet from its wearer, you have a chance to destroy it and stop the shield guardian in its tracks.

WARFORGED

LAIR Warforged are found across Eberron, an ancient world with twelve moons where science and magic are intertwined. Many still reside in Khorvaire, where the Last War took place, but some have chosen to explore distant regions. Their homes tend to be functional rather than decorative, reflecting their military origins.

SIZE A warforged's size depends on what it was built to do, although most have the build of a tall, muscular human. A warforged designed to infiltrate and spy might be much smaller than is typical, while one intended to smash through walls and other defenses may have added bulk.

WARFORGED NAMES

The warforged were originally identified by a string of numbers rather than by individual names. Many still use the nicknames they were given by comrades during the war, while others have chosen new monikers for themselves. A few take on human names to honor a fallen friend or mentor. Typical warforged names include Blue, Crunch, Dent, Five, Hammer, Lucky, Rusty, Scout, and Temple.

Warforged are made of wood and steel, but they feel pain and emotion like any sentient creature. Created as mindless automatons to fight in the Last War on the world of Eberron, an unexpected breakthrough made these constructs fully self-aware. Built as weapons, the warforged must now find a purpose beyond the battle.

All warforged share a common facial design with a hinged jaw, crystal eyes, and a unique magic sigil on their foreheads. Their bodies have rootlike cords that function as muscles, wrapped around a tough framework and protected by armored plates. Other aspects of their design vary based on their original wartime role. Warforged can range from huge juggernauts made of heavy steel to lithe fighters crafted from wood and featherweight mithral.

Warforged rarely show emotion, whatever they are feeling. Most seek out a concrete purpose to replace the structure they lost when the war ended. A few embrace their freedom, exploring their moods, creativity, and spiritual interests. As living humanoids, the warforged still benefit from resting, healing magic, and medicine. They don't need to eat, drink, breathe, or sleep, and they are resistant to poison and immune to disease.

DO THIS	DON'T DO THIS
Be patient. Many warforged struggle to understand social customs and may behave in strange or inappropriate ways.	**Don't be vague.** Warforged prefer clear, precise communication. Meandering stories or confusing directions will just irritate them.
Talk to them. Unlike other constructs, you might be able to persuade a warforged to help in your quest—or at least to not fight *you*.	**Don't treat them like robots.** Despite their metal parts, warforged aren't machines that you can order around.

THE LORD OF BLADES

5

Many of the warforged emerged from the Last War with a hatred for battle and a desire to find new purpose, but a few struggled to adapt and still longed for another war to fight. After all, warforged were created for battle and these wanted to fulfill their design. A leader emerged to answer that call: the Lord of Blades. Some say he was a fighter in the war who had adopted a new identity. Others claim he was the last warforged to be made. Whatever his origins, he quickly gained a reputation as a terrifying and brutal figure.

The Lord of Blades hopes to create a warforged nation. He is building an army and gathering weapons and magic for a planned campaign to destroy or imprison all living things. There are many who would like to stop him, but few with the courage to face him.

LAIR The land of Cyre was devastated by the war, with few survivors. The Lord of Blades claims this region as his own and sends his soldiers to patrol the wastelands, slaughtering any who venture into the territory. Some adventurers will take the risk since many weapons and items of power lay scattered across his domain. Many more of these magic items have already fallen into the grasp of the Lord of Blades.

SIZE The Lord of Blades is the size of a very tall human man. His blades and bladed wings make him appear even bigger and more imposing.

TOO MANY BLADES

There's no mystery about how the Lord of Blades got his name. His reinforced armor is covered with blades that can cut anyone who comes close. The bladed wings on his back are useless for flying but very effective for slashing. He also carries a weapon called the *sixblade*, a staff with three long blades at either end. In a single attack, he can strike with his wings as well as both ends of the deadly weapon.

On top of all that, the Lord of Blades is a formidable spellcaster. Even if you manage to stay out of his blade's reach, he may hit you with a damaging spell, like *fire bolt* or *thunderwave*.

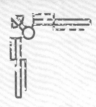
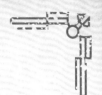

ARTIFICERS

Vi had been thrown in a few prisons in her day, and even banished from a few places, but this was the first time she could remember being trapped in a scrap-heap dimension. She had come to the Sword Coast to confront a wizard about crimes against peace, and he had sent her flying through a portal into the same dump to which he sent all his old shield guardians, and, somehow, he was blocking Vi's ability to walk between planes.

There was nothing here to help the artificer except dormant constructs made of wood and metal, and a few cracked and broken magic amulets that could once have controlled these constructs. There was no obvious exit. But Vi wasn't worried. She was certain that she had enough raw materials—and enough magic—to build a way out. Then she would see about confronting that wizard.

The way an adventurer uses magic often reflects the way they see the universe and how they hope to make sense of its secrets. For artificers, the universe is an elaborate puzzle they want to solve, and magic is about creating the right tools to solve it. In these pages, you'll learn all about the artificer class, the specializations available to artificers, and the spells or "infusions" they rely on.

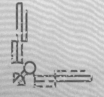
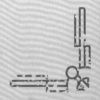

ARTIFICER CLASS OVERVIEW

ARE YOU ALWAYS TRYING TO
FIGURE OUT HOW THINGS WORK?

DO YOU SURROUND YOURSELF
WITH TOOLS AND TOYS?

DO YOU LIKE TO TINKER, BUILD,
AND INVENT?

YOU MIGHT BE AN ARTIFICER!

A rtificers are inventors who harness magic through their creations. They experiment with elixirs, tinker with gadgets, and build enchanted armor and weapons to unlock the magical mysteries of the world. All their magic is channeled through their use of tools, so, to the eyes of others, artificers' spells are often indistinguishable from science. Artificers are motivated by a hunger for discovery. They want to invent something original, create a new element, or discover some strange natural phenomenon. Their ingenuity makes them highly sought after as alchemists, weaponsmiths, and even field medics.

MOVING BETWEEN WORLDS

Artificers might be happy to stay in their workshops if it were not for their compulsive curiosity, which drives them to pursue adventures in other cities, nations, and realms. Some artificers have found ways to travel between worlds using portals or spelljammer ships. Networks of artificers exist across the multiverse to share their incredible discoveries.

EQUIPMENT AND ATTRIBUTES

Armor: Most artificers favor light- or medium-weight armor with defensive enchantments, but some are proud to build the most impressive suits of armor you've ever seen.

Weapons: Artificers favor simple weapons because their real power comes from the magic infused in their equipment. Some artificers don't bother with traditional weapons at all, enjoying the challenge of turning ordinary items into a magical arsenal.

Magic of Artifice: Artificers don't use spellbooks to cast spells. All their magic comes from using tools to change an object or material.

Infuse Items: Artificers can store spells in objects to create their own magic artifacts (see page 78).

SPECIALIZATIONS

All artificers share some fascination with how things work, but their curiosity takes them in very different directions. Some are called to combat. Others are more comfortable in workshops. After learning the essentials of their field, artificers usually fall into one of four specializations and develop the unique talents that come from that area of expertise: alchemists, armorers, artillerists, and battle smiths.

ALCHEMISTS

If you love conducting experiments and watching strange liquids bubble in glass jars, the life of an alchemist may be for you. Alchemists are the original artificers, using their study of ordinary and extraordinary materials to tap into magical effects, including those that can extend a life or cut one short. Most alchemists spend a lot of time in a lab—or something very similar to a lab but more suited to their interests, like a classroom, library, or kitchen.

Experienced alchemists can choose a bottle or flask to magically fill with a magical elixir that has different helpful effects every time someone drinks it. Sometimes the liquid heals, other times it makes the drinker faster, tougher, braver, or allows them to fly or change shape. Unfortunately, this elixir is unstable and it's almost impossible to predict the effects.

Healing and long life are at the heart of the alchemist's art, but for every healing effect they uncover, they're likely to also find some outcome that can be used as a weapon, perhaps even to drain the lifeforce from an enemy.

ARMORERS

If you're not the toughest, strongest, or quickest adventurer, but you don't want that to hold you back from the action, the armorer specialty may be perfect for you. Armorers use their tinkering skills and knowledge of magic to create unique suits of armor to match their needs, allowing them to strike hard or move fast.

Armorers have access to a number of long-range attack spells as well as spells that distract or trick their opponents. Their enchanted armor becomes a second skin, providing benefits to the entire body and replacing missing limbs, if desired. The armorer can take the armor on and off in an instant, but no one else can remove it.

Artificer armor can switch between two major modes: guardian mode and infiltrator mode. In guardian mode, the armor has a defensive field and gauntlets that deliver thunder-powered punches. In infiltrator mode, the armor makes the wearer stealthier, faster, and more nimble, with a special weapon that can fire lightning blasts. Experienced armorers can infuse different parts of their armor with spells as an additional boost. Imagine a visor that allows you to see through invisibility spells, or boots that allow you to step through the air, or a chest plate that bounces back any strikes against it.

ARTILLERISTS

If you like making things explode, an artillerist may be the specialization for you. Artillerists are experts at creating long-range and destructive weapons, so they're highly sought after by military forces. Many of their preferred spells are devastating long-range attacks, so a few artillerists on the battlefield can make a big difference.

One of the first artificer crafts that an artillerist will perfect is making an *eldritch cannon*, a projectile weapon that can be small enough to hold in one hand or big enough to stand on its own working legs. The design of the cannon is up to the artillerist, as is the magical effect it produces. Some cannons shoot a cone of fire. Some project blasts of powerful force. Some emit a healing ray that can benefit your entire adventuring party.

Experienced artillerists can turn a wand, staff, or other handheld wooden object into a conduit for destructive spells by carving sigils into the surface. This means an artillerist could turn a wooden spoon or a broken chair leg into an arcane weapon in a moment of need. Though the artillerist's gifts of magic are largely destructive, not all artillerists want to cause devastation. Their weapons can be used to protect or fortify a location or to provide covering fire for travelers.

BATTLE SMITH

Like artillerists, battle smiths often find themselves in the heat of combat, but their specialization is designed to help people in trouble. Artificers who are especially brave and selfless are often called to this role. Battle smiths are usually protectors and medics who rush into conflict to help the injured and repair the broken. Their preferred spells offer protection, courage, and healing, and they are often gifted fighters. Battle smiths have one other significant advantage: the steel defender.

A steel defender is a battle smith's companion, a mechanical assistant of the artificer's own design. A steel defender moves when the battle smith moves and follows their commands. The defender can also pull their battle smith out of the fray when injured. Steel defenders are well armored, well armed, and always on watch; they don't get tired and can't be poisoned. They will attempt to deflect attacks against all members of their party, and they can even be self-healing.

Battle smiths are not helpless without their defenders, of course. They have their own spells and talents, and many of them learn how to channel arcane energy to harm or heal with a single strike.

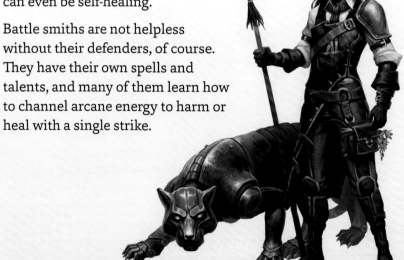

AN UNCOMFORTABLE RESCUE

Berli Boldstrom could hardly remember his name when he awoke in the snow, let alone where he was or why he was there. All he knew was that he was very cold, and he wanted to go back to sleep. As Berli closed his eyes, his memories took shape. He was looking for something. A book. A manual to stir a golem to life. He and his friends planned to steal that book from a lonely old alchemist living on Mount Elva. The golem was their best hope to rebuild their island home after a devastating storm.

But why was Berli in the snow? He vaguely recalled a frost giant who seemed to come from nowhere and had picked Berli up by his foot and flung him over the treetops. Berli was thinking how lucky he was to survive the fall as he drifted back to sleep.

He did not sleep for long. Something clamped on to his leg and dragged him out of the snow. Berli feared that the giant had found him. Instead, he looked up into the sympathetic face of a human woman— and the metal dog creature gently holding Berli's leg with its mouth.

"You're safe," said the woman. "My name is Jhonna, and this is my companion, Spoons. I'm a battle mage. I'll take you up the hill to my father. He's an alchemist. He can warm you up and make you fit for your travels."

Berli just nodded, unsure what to say—or what to do.

Berli has escaped a brush with death and been invited into the home of the alchemist whom he planned to rob. Can he abandon his friends to the frost giant, and can he justify stealing from the people who saved his life? What would you do in this situation?

ARTIFICER INFUSIONS

One of the amazing abilities that artificers have that sets them apart from other character classes is the ability to take an ordinary object and infuse it with magic properties. An artificer who is just starting out might infuse a sword or a crossbow to make it more powerful, or infuse a piece of armor so that it offers greater protection. As artificers gain experience and skill, they can create more powerful and unusual infusions.

Novice artificers can infuse up to two items at the same time, while a very experienced artificer may infuse and carry up to six seemingly ordinary objects with magic effects. Here are some infusions from which an artificer can choose.

ARMOR OF MAGICAL STRENGTH This infusion allows the armor's wearer to temporarily increase their strength or stay on their feet when an attack would have knocked them down.

BOOTS OF THE WINDING PATH Any pair of boots or shoes with this infusion can be used to instantly return the wearer to the place they just came from. It's perfect for a quick retreat or for getting out of some traps.

HELM OF AWARENESS The wearer of this helmet has a heightened sense of their surroundings. They cannot be surprised, and they have a better chance of leading the action in combat.

MIND SHARPENER If a spell requires intense concentration, or if a person is exhausted from travel and worried about making a mistake, a robe or piece of armor with this infusion will provide a sudden jolt that pushes the wearer into a more focused state of mind.

REPLICATE MAGIC ITEM This is possibly the most useful infusion, and certainly the most versatile. Artificers can create a version of any common magic item so long as they have the required level of expertise and experience. They don't need access to the original item, just an ordinary object of similar form. For example, an artificer could use this infusion to create *darkvision goggles*, a *wand of magic detection*, a hat that disguises the wearer, or winged boots.

RETURNING WEAPON If an adventurer has a favorite weapon that can be thrown, like a dagger or a spear, this infusion ensures that the weapon will always return to its wielder.

COMPANIONS

Vi is always accompanied by her homunculus, Aura, a foxlike winged construct that often sits on her shoulder. When traveling between worlds, Vi may also bring along a heavily armored warforged soldier to act as her bodyguard.

The gnome artificer known as Vi was a weaponsmith during the Last War on Eberron. She helped create the cannons, bombs, and warforged soldiers that caused so much devastation. When the war ended, Vi looked at the world she had helped destroy and decided she needed to start fixing the damage she had caused—not just in her own world but in every realm that needed her help.

Vi created an organization called the Fixers, a group of adventurers and artificers who confront the problems that only skilled artificers might hope to repair. Thanks to a special mark on her skin that allows her to travel between planes, Vi visits various worlds to establish local Fixer offices and share her wisdom and discoveries with other artificers. She is motivated by a strong desire to make up for past mistakes but also by her endless fascination with exploration and discovery.

PLAYING VI Vi is a brilliant inventor with years of experience on both sides of war, first in making weapons and then in creating opportunities for peace. A natural problem-solver and an excellent teacher, Vi takes other adventurers under her wing to help them change their worlds for the better. She has a great sense of humor, but beneath her wisecracks she is an intensely thoughtful person.

CRISPY

Vi carries an arcane cannon that takes the form of an ornate brass cockatrice—a creature that is part chicken, part dragon. This cannon shoots a long plume of flame that sets everything in its path on fire, earning it the nickname "Crispy." In an emergency, Vi can detonate the cannon like a bomb—but then she will need to build another Crispy.

HOMUNCULUS SERVANTS

SPECIAL POWERS

CHANNEL MAGIC
An artificer can transmit a touch-based spell via their homunculus if the homunculus is close by.

FORCED STRIKE
A homunculus can ram an enemy at speed on its artificer's command.

IMMUNITY
Like most constructs, homunculi are immune to poison and fatigue.

An artificer's best friend is their homunculus. Both an infusion and a construct, a homunculus is an artificial being brought to life by a magic gemstone or crystal to act as a companion and assistant to an artificer. To create a homunculus, an artificer must infuse a valuable stone with the appropriate enchantment. The stone becomes the heart of the new creation, while its body takes shape from other materials, such as scraps of metal.

The artificer chooses their homunculus's appearance, so it might take the form of a mechanical animal, like a lizard or a falcon, or it could take the form of an object, like a cauldron or a tea kettle. Whatever the shape, homunculi can fly using wings or other means of momentum, like rotor blades or propulsive jets.

A homunculus is a loyal assistant to the artificer who created it and will follow their commands to the best of its ability. Homunculi can understand their creator's language, but they cannot speak. When not given any instructions, a homunculus will do its best to stay out of trouble and dodge attacks. If destroyed, the homunculus's body will disappear, but its gemstone will remain so that the artificer can hopefully revive it in the future.

SIZE Homunculi are generally small. They are rarely bigger than a house cat or a parrot and are sometimes little enough to fit in a pocket or satchel.

DO THIS	DON'T DO THIS
Be respectful. An artificer's homunculus is a member of the adventuring party.	**Don't get in the way.** A busy homunculus is probably working on important tasks for its creator, who won't appreciate delays.
Protect their heart. If a homunculus is destroyed, make sure to save its gemstone.	**Don't underestimate them.** Though not powerful itself, a homunculus might be carrying a powerful spell.

DESIGNING YOUR OWN MAGIC ITEMS

"So you can put spells right into my lute?" the bard squeaked excitedly. Before Zakaron could reply, the bard continued, "Oh, where should I even start? What about a spell to charm my listeners? No, my music already does that. Maybe *magic missile*? Or *fireball*? That's always impressive!"

Zakaron ducked away from the wildly swinging instrument and spoke calmly, trying to temper his new client's expectations. "Impressively expensive and time-consuming, you mean," he responded. "Perhaps we could start with some light, healing magic instead?"

The boundless possibilities of magic objects provide a great space to explore your creativity and imagination. In these pages, you'll learn techniques for creating new items to include in your game, how to deal with cursed things, and ways that characters can make magic devices in-game.

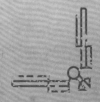

MAGIC ITEM TRAITS

Before you get started on creating your own unique magic items, it's helpful to keep in mind a few traits that can affect how such objects are used in DUNGEONS & DRAGONS.

ATTUNEMENT

Many magic items, especially powerful ones, need to be attuned to their user. This process involves sitting quietly with the object to create a magical bond between you and the artifact. This bond lasts until you decide to break it, except in the case of cursed items (see page 98) and some sentient items (see page 11).

Some magic items are selective about which users can attune to them. For instance, a magic wand might only attune with wizards or sorcerers, or an enchanted bow might require you to already know archery. You can only be attuned to three magic items at a time, so choose wisely.

CATEGORIES

Every magic item belongs to one of nine categories: armor, potions, rings, rods, scrolls, staffs, wands, weapons, or wondrous items. An item's category can give clues about how it works. For example, staffs and wands often have charges (see following), while potions and scrolls are consumable objects that can only be used once. "Wondrous" is a catchall category that includes worn magic items other than armor and rings, along with bags, carpets, figurines, musical instruments, and any other enchanted object.

CHARGES

A charge is a stored bit of magic energy that is depleted when an object's power is activated. This places a limit on how often the item can be used, since without this spark, its powers can't be activated. Some enchanted items can regain charges over time. Items that don't recharge become nonmagical or may even be destroyed once the final charge is expended.

RARITY

Magic items can be grouped into five loose categories based on their rarity: common, uncommon, rare, very rare, and legendary. Typically, the rarer an item, the greater its power and value. Beyond these five categories are "artifacts," unique items of exceptional power whose very existence may trigger world-changing events.

MODIFYING MAGIC ITEMS

The quickest way to invent a new magic item is to adjust a premade one. This saves you some time by letting you use existing rules and item statistics, while adding something special to your adventure.

ADD PERSONALITY AND HISTORY

A generic magic sword that does additional cold damage is neat, but not especially memorable. That same sword carved with dwarven runes from a lost Northern Kingdom that glow under the full moon's light, warning of a great battle yet to come? That's a sword worthy of a bardic tune. By adding details such as an item's name, origin, decoration, and quirks, you can transform a basic magic object into something truly unique and fun.

ALTER THE ITEM'S ABILITIES

Many magic items cause certain types of damage, such as cold, fire, lightning, piercing, or slashing. Changing the damage type—such as making a flame sword do lightning damage instead of fire—is an easy way to keep things surprising.

CHANGE THE ITEM TYPE

A magic axe can just as easily become a mace, sword, or dagger with the same abilities and requirements. A protective ring could become a cloak, necklace, or belt, or a wand's magic could instead appear in a staff or a circlet.

COMBINE ITEMS

Merging the properties of two different enchanted objects is a quick method to create a powerful, versatile magic item. For example, you could combine *boots of speed* with a magic *prosthetic limb* to create a replacement limb that lets the wearer move with short bursts of fantastic fleetness.

LIMIT USAGE

If you want to include a powerful magic item without making things too easy for your adventurers, you can add usage limits to ensure the object isn't wielded to resolve every situation. Perhaps the item only regains charges once a week or month, rather than once a day, or maybe it breaks after a few uses. Another way to do this is by changing the item into the single-use format of a potion or scroll.

CREATING NEW ITEMS

When it comes to designing all-new magic items, the only real limit is your imagination. Almost any object can be imbued with magic, from ordinary things to one-of-a-kind relics. While adventurers tend to favor what will be useful on their quests—weapons, armor, healing properties, and powers of movement—there's no reason to restrict your inventions to those categories.

The functionality of most magic items falls into two broad camps: those that improve a character's existing abilities, and those that let them access an entirely new ability. Examples of the first type are weapons that improve a fighter's ability to hit and damage opponents, shoes that let rogues move soundlessly, or a jeweled pendant that enhances a spellcaster's magic skills. The second group includes items such as a ring that lets you levitate, a shield that makes you resistant to poisoning, or a hat that lets you speak a language that you've never learned.

Your original magic items can take either approach, or even be combined for an object of greater power. Bear in mind that the more powers an item has, the harder it will be for your adventuring party to remember and use them all. This is especially true when those powers are wildly different. A helmet that makes you invisible, casts healing spells, transforms into a boat, and produces cookies on command sounds awesome, but keeping track of all those powers can become a distraction instead of adding to your story.

It's important to keep a balance between the power level of your new magic item and the challenges that the adventurers face. A magic item that automatically defeats every opponent would take the risk and excitement out of your game, while one that's almost never useful won't feel like much of a reward for players.

WHO DECIDES?

New magic items are typically introduced into the game by the Dungeon Master (DM), the person responsible for creating the world and the story where the characters exist. Players can also suggest ideas for new items, although the final decision on including these objects—and any hidden or unexpected quirks—is up to the DM.

The same goes for crafting magic items in-game. Even if a character has the skills, knowledge, and resources to make an item, the DM may reject ideas that would be too powerful or otherwise wrong for the story you're all telling together. One good compromise as DM is to allow the item but add restrictions (see Limit Usage, page 89) that will keep players from using it in every situation.

CRAFTING ITEMS IN-GAME

While magic items are typically acquired during a quest, either as treasure or as a reward, characters can attempt to craft new objects as well. This process requires time, effort, and materials, along with a formula explaining the steps and spellcasting ability needed to create the device. Because of the effort involved, creating magic items happens during downtime, the break that characters take between adventures to refresh, retrain, and relax.

Magic items may require one or more exotic ingredients, such as a dragon scale, snakeskin from a medusa, or coal from a fire giant's forge. These ingredients often relate to the item's intended effect. For example, creating a *ring of regeneration* might call for the hair of a troll or other creature with regenerative abilities. Finding these materials can be an adventure all on its own!

Once you've collected all your materials and tools, you're ready to start crafting. Depending on the complexity and power level of your desired object, the time required can vary from one week for common items to a full year for a legendary item. You'll also need to have saved up your loot, since you can expect to spend two thousand gold coins when making a rare magic item or even one hundred thousand gold coins on an item of legendary quality.

For every five weeks that you spend working on crafting a magic item, there's a chance of encountering a complication. Some are merely annoying, like local gossip or needing to replace a stolen tool. Other impediments may put your work at risk, such as when a powerful noble insists that the item be given to them once it's complete.

BREWING POTIONS

If you opt to create consumable magic items, like potions or scrolls, you can save half the time and cost of producing a more durable object. This can be useful if you're on a tight budget or schedule.

Potions of healing are a special category and can be created by anyone capable of using an herbalism kit. A basic healing potion takes one day to create and costs twenty-five gold coins for ingredients. More powerful healing potions can be achieved by dedicating one to four weeks of time and between one hundred and ten thousand gold coins. Many alchemists, healers, priests, and spellcasters offer basic healing potions for sale, although they may charge a high price or even require favors instead of gold as payment.

CRAFTING MAGIC ITEMS

During their adventures in the dungeons of Undermountain, half-orc barbarian Urnath lost her left forearm during a particularly hard fight. Urnath's new prosthetic limb was working well, but her wizard companion, Puknik, hoped to make her something exceptional. Seeking advice, he sailed along the Dessarin River to the city of Yartar, where his teacher, Ardreth the Astute, resided.

"What I have in mind is a prosthetic limb infused with the same magic as a weapon of warning," Puknik said.

"It might be possible," replied Ardreth. "I can find the necessary formula but, in exchange, you'll owe me a favor. You'll also need a scale from a crystal dragon, which won't be easy to secure, and the work itself will take at least half a year."

Seeing Puknik's hesitation, his mentor continued. "I do have the formula for *gauntlets of flaming fury* on hand, which would adapt more easily. All you'd need would be the shed skin of a fire snake and a couple of weeks."

Urnath would be pretty happy to punch things with a flaming fist, Puknik thought, but she was already great at punching things. A magic item that alerted her to nearby danger would give her a completely different ability. Puknik realized this wasn't a decision he could make on his own. "Let me discuss it with Urnath and I'll let you know."

Should Urnath and Puknik take the straightforward path suggested by Ardreth, or accept the extra work of crafting Puknik's original concept? If the latter, will the Dungeon Master place any limits on how the finished item works? What plot opportunities can be created using the favor they now owe to Puknik's mentor? Will any complications arise during the process of crafting the magic item? The choices are yours!

GLYPHS AND WARDS

Glyphs and wards are special symbols invested with magic power that activate when specific conditions are met. They can be inscribed on physical spaces or objects, letting you create temporary or permanent enchanted effects when triggered. As a general rule, you can remember the difference between glyphs and wards this way:

GLYPHS ARE OFFENSIVE
They explode, usually catching their victims off guard.

WARDS ARE DEFENSIVE
They're used to protect a space from outside interference.

GLYPH OF WARDING SCHOOL: ABJURATION

This third-level spell—available to bards, clerics, wizards, and artificers—lets you inscribe a glyph on a surface or within an object that can be closed, like a book or chest. This symbol must be smaller than ten square feet and is almost completely invisible. You can set conditions for how the glyph is triggered, such as by touch or a specific sound, as well as conditions that will *not* set it off.

Once unleashed, the glyph either explodes with one of five kinds of damage—acid, fire, frost, lightning, or thunder—or unleashes a stored spell. This stored spell is usually damaging, such as *magic missile*, although beneficial spells, like *cure wounds*, can also be stored in a glyph.

SPELL TIPS

- A well-placed glyph can help keep a wizard's spellbook safe from thieves or other casters who want to steal the research.

- A careful and clever observer might be able to detect the presence of a glyph, but just noticing the symbol isn't enough to deactivate its effects.

GUARDS AND WARDS

SCHOOL: ABJURATION

Bards and wizards can learn this sixth-level spell that lets you create a warded space of up to twenty-five-hundred square feet, about the size of a tennis court. This warded area can be up to twenty feet tall and take any shape you like, so long as all the spaces connect. When casting the spell, you can choose which adventurers will be unaffected or set a password that will make the speaker immune to the ward's effects.

Once triggered, the warded area fills with fog, and stairwells are covered in magic cobwebs that hamper movement. All doors magically lock, and up to ten doors are disguised to look like normal walls. Wards remain in place for up to twenty-four hours from when they are cast.

SPELL TIPS

- Other illusions or magic effects can be added to a warded area, including spooky sounds, gusts of wind, dancing lights, or clouds of stinking smoke.

- If a spellcaster casts this incantation on the same location every single day for a full year (365 days), the ward becomes permanent.

CURSED ITEMS

A cursed magic item inflicts a negative effect on its user, along with any benefits the object may have. It's never fun to discover that your shiny new magic trinket comes with a hefty burden. Such objects can be difficult to detect. Most methods of discovering an item's powers, including the *identify* spell, won't reveal if an object is cursed. Even attuning an item won't immediately reveal if it carries a jinx. Adventurers have been known to use a magic item for days, months, or even years before discovering its true nature.

In some cases, you may need to use an item a certain number of times before the curse is activated. In others, the effect may be so subtle that you don't initially notice any problem. A cursed necklace that burns your skin whenever you take it off is obvious, but one that makes all your wounds take twice as long to heal will be harder to figure out.

Breaking a curse is no easy task. Unlike with normal magic items, you can't just decide to end your attunement with a cursed device. The *remove curse* spell will usually free you from the hex magic, allowing you to discard the item, but the object itself will remain cursed. To break an especially strong curse, you may need to undertake a quest that involves seeking out special ingredients, resolving unfinished conflicts, or accomplishing other difficult tasks.

CURSE EXAMPLES

Curses can take many forms, although they often invert the benefits provided by the item's magic in some way. For example:

Armor that offers additional protection to one type of damage—but makes you even more vulnerable to a different type.

A lucky stone that makes it easier to accomplish one task—but harder to do the next two things you attempt.

A thrown weapon that always returns to your hand—but sometimes hurts you when it comes back.

A cloak that lets you change shape into a monstrous form—but doesn't always let you change back.

A magic orb that lets you see in the dark—but extinguishes all flames within thirty feet of you.

What other ideas for cursed items can you imagine?

DESTROYING MAGIC ITEMS

Most magic items are works of remarkable craft, made from the finest materials with careful attention paid to every detail. They are at least as durable as an ordinary item of the same kind, and many magic objects are designed to be impervious to any and all kinds of damage. That's good news for those you want to keep, but what about dangerous ones you might need to destroy?

Demolishing a magic item typically involves a quest, often a long and difficult one. Your goal may require reaching a mythical forge, a bottomless cavern, or even another plane of existence in order to shatter the item's physical form. Other objects may need to be reunited with the remains of their creator or accomplish one last task before their power will disperse. A holy location or divine relic may be needed to break the magic of an evil item, or you might have to source a dozen rare ingredients to free a soul imprisoned within an enchanted object. The possibilities are as boundless as your imagination.

SHORT-TERM SOLUTIONS

If you're not quite ready to take on the complex quest of destroying a magic item, there are some temporary ways you can restrict its powers.

ANTI-MAGIC FIELD A very high-level spell, *anti-magic field* creates a ten-foot circle around the caster where all magic effects are suppressed. Magic items within this field function as normal objects of the same type, and magic effects created outside the zone will dissipate upon touching the field's edge.

DISPEL MAGIC This mid-level spell lets you try to stop a magic effect of equal (or less) potency from continuing to affect your target. This isn't effective against powerful magic effects, like curses, but can help against more common ones.

SELL OR TRADE IT Finding a buyer or seller for magic items is a tricky business. Con artists and thieves abound, meaning legitimate dealers will be cautious about accepting enchanted objects from a new source. Despite the challenges, this can be a good solution for replacing unneeded magic items with more useful ones—or a hefty sack of gold.

UN-ATTUNE THE ITEM Many magic items only work when attuned to someone. Removing your attunement will temporarily keep the item's magic from activating. However, this does leave the object vulnerable to being attuned by anyone else who happens to pick it up. In some cases, like cursed or sentient items, voluntarily breaking your attunement may not even be an option.

USING MAGIC ITEMS
TO TELL YOUR OWN STORIES

Billi heard tromping footsteps and the familiar snarl of Goblin words echoing down the hall. She knew she had only a moment before the guards would round the corner and catch her. She reached into the pocket of her tunic and pulled out a flat piece of iron covered in faint whirling mystic symbols. Clipper told her this enchanted immovable rod was simple to operate—just put it where you want, tap the button, and, in theory, it would lock in place.

With a couple quick steps, Billi ran toward the nearest wall, using momentum and all the leg strength she could muster to vault into the air. When she felt her body hit the peak of the jump, she whispered a tiny prayer and pressed the button.

Incredibly, it worked. The magic rod completely stopped and held firm in midair. Billi gripped the strange metal handle with all her might and tried not to make any noise while a pair of hobgoblins in rusty armor wandered through the hallway, completely unaware the slippery thief for whom they were looking hung directly above them.

Magic items and places are at the heart of some of the most famous fantasy stories ever told. Combining magic and the mundane is an irresistible mix that engages and entertains audiences all over the world.

Every fantasy story starts with a simple idea—an object or a location, a character with a mission and a desire to go somewhere new. It's the same process that authors and designers use when they come up with the fantasy stories that you read in books or graphic novels, watch on TV or in the movies, or play in tabletop and video games. Every story starts with a single spark and grows in unexpected ways. If you write down your ideas and refine them, you can build a unique fantasy adventure all your own. Here are some questions to jump-start your brainstorming:

WHAT IS THE ITEM CALLED?

- Give your creation a name that's memorable and descriptive. "The Sage Stone, Heart of Cormyr" tells everyone that this object is something worthy of adventure.

WHO WANTS IT?

- Imagine a villain who also seeks this item. Do they want to control it, destroy it, or does it carry some other secret linked to the villain's past?

HOW DOES ITS MAGIC MANIFEST?

- Give your magic object interesting features that activate your senses. Does it glow with unearthly light from within? Does it give off a peculiar sound or smell?

WHY DOES IT EXIST?

- Invent a backstory for your magic device. Where did it come from? Who built it? Does it have a special purpose?

WHEN COULD ITS MAGIC CHANGE?

- Is the item cursed and, if so, why? What would it take to purify or corrupt it? Can it be broken, or is it invulnerable?

Remember, you don't have to answer all these questions by yourself! DUNGEONS & DRAGONS is a collaborative game where you work with your friends to create your own stories. Even if you're the Dungeon Master, setting the scene and describing places and threats in the mystical world, each player should contribute to the story as well. Leave some mysteries still to be discovered and incorporate ideas from your players so everyone feels connected as the tale grows, bit by bit.

If you don't feel confident creating a brand-new enchanted quest from scratch, that's okay! Don't be afraid to use pieces from this book or elements from other books, shows, or games that you've enjoyed. It's fine to draw inspiration from all kinds of sources, especially when you're building stories for fun.

After you've read through all the wondrous things in this guide, look for additional DUNGEONS & DRAGONS material to ignite your imagination. The other Young Adventurer's Guides are bursting with characters, creatures, skills, spells, and so much more. Your knowledge of artifacts and the arcane has grown, so venture forth with confidence and *explore the unknown!*

Published in the United States by Ten Speed Press, an imprint of the Crown Publishing Group, a division of Penguin Random House LLC, New York.
TenSpeed.com

Ten Speed Press and the Ten Speed Press colophon are registered trademarks of Penguin Random House LLC.

Some of the illustrations in this work have been previously published.

Typefaces: Capita by Dieter Hofrichter, IMB Plex Sans by Mike Abbink, Johnstemp by Georg John, Tiamat Condensed by Jim Parkinson, and Tiamat Text by Jim Parkinson

Library of Congress Cataloging-in-Publication Data

Names: Zub, Jim author. | King, Stacy, author. | Wheeler, Andrew, 1976- author.
Title: Artificers & alchemy : a young adventurer's guide / written by Jim Zub and Stacy King, with Andrew Wheeler.
Description: First edition. | California ; New York : Ten Speed Press, [2024] | Series: Dungeons & Dragons young adventurer's guides
Identifiers: LCCN 2023026980 (print) | LCCN 2023026981 (ebook) | ISBN 9781984862204 (hardcover) | ISBN 9781984862211 (ebook)
Subjects: LCSH: Dungeons and Dragons (Game)
Classification: LCC GV1469.62.D84 Z827 2024 (print) | LCC GV1469.62.D84 (ebook) | DDC 793.93--dc23/eng/20230920
LC record available at https://lccn.loc.gov/2023026980
LC ebook record available at https://lccn.loc.gov/2023026981

Hardcover ISBN: 978-1-9848-6220-4
eBook ISBN: 978-1-9848-6221-1

Printed in China

Publisher: Aaron Wehner
Acquiring editor: Shaida Boroumand | Project editor: Zoey Brandt | Production editor: Natalie Blachere
Designer: Betsy Stromberg | Production designer: Claudia Sanchez
Production manager: Dan Myers
Copyeditor: Amy Smith Bell | Proofreader: Michael Fedison
Publicist: Maya Bradford | Marketer: Paola Crespo
Illustrators: Goodname Digital Art Studio

10 9 8 7 6 5 4 3 2 1

First Edition